HE

BOOKS BY ROBERT A. JOHNSON

He: Understanding Masculine Psychology
Revised Edition

She: Understanding Feminine Psychology
Revised Edition

We: Understanding the Psychology of Romantic
Love

Inner Work: Using Dreams & Active Imagination
for Personal Growth

Ecstasy: Understanding the Psychology of Joy

HE

Understanding Masculine Psychology

Revised Edition

ROBERT A. JOHNSON

HARPER ● PERENNIAL

NEW YORK ● LONDON ● TORONTO ● SYDNEY

This revised edition is published by arrangement with Mills House, P.O. Box 8147, Berkeley, California, 94707.

REVISED EDITION

Library of Congress Cataloging-in-Publication Data

Johnson, Robert A., 1921–
  He : understanding masculine psychology / Robert A. Johnson.—
Rev. ed.
    p. cm.
  ISBN 0-06-055178-X
  ISBN 0-06-096396-4 (pbk.)
    1. Men--Psychology. 2. Chrétien, de Troyes, 12th cent. Perceval
le Gallois. I. Title.
BF692.5.J63 1989
155.3'32—dc20   89-45097

89 90 91 92 93 RRD 10 9 8 7 6 5 4 3 2 1

17 18 19 LSC-C 58 57 56 55   (pbk.)

Contents

Introduction   ix

The Fisher King   1

Parsifal   13

Chastity   31

The Grail Castle   43

The Dry Years   59

The Hideous Damsel   67

The Long Quest   73

Suggestions for Further Reading   83

Introduction

Often, when a new era begins in history, a myth for that era springs up simultaneously. The myth is a preview of what is to come, and it contains sage advice for coping with the psychological elements of the time.

In the myth of Parsifal's search for the Holy Grail we have such a prescription for our modern day. The Grail myth arose in the twelfth century, a time when many people feel that our modern age began; ideas, attitudes and concepts we are living with today had their beginnings in the days when the Grail myth took form. One can say that the winds of the twelfth century have become the whirlwinds of the twentieth century.

The theme of the Grail myth was much in evidence in the twelfth, thirteenth, and fourteenth centuries. We will be using the French version, which is the earliest written account, taken from a poem by

Chrétien de Troyes. There is also a German version by Wolfram von Eschenbach. The English version, *Le Morte Darthur* by Thomas Malory, comes from the fourteenth century; but by that time it had been elaborated a great deal. The French version is simpler, more direct and nearer to the unconscious; therefore it is more helpful for our purposes.

We must remember that a myth is a living entity, and exists within every person. You will get the true, living form of the myth if you can see it as it spins away inside yourself. The most rewarding mythological experience you can have is to see how it lives in your own psychological structure.

The Grail myth speaks of masculine psychology. This is not to say that it is confined to the male, for a woman participates in her own inner masculinity, though it is less dominant for her. We must take everything that goes into the myth as part of ourselves. We will have to cope with a dazzling array of fair damsels, but must see them too as parts of the masculine psyche. Women, too, will be interested in the secrets of the Grail myth, for every woman has to cope with one of these exotic creatures, the male of the species, somehow, as father, or husband, or son. Also a woman partakes quite directly of the Grail myth as the story of her own interior masculinity. Especially as modern women take more part in the masculine world by embracing a profession, the development of masculinity becomes important to her. A woman's masculinity or a man's femininity is closer than one realizes. The insights of this myth will be immediate and practical for our present time.

The Fisher King

Our story begins with the Grail castle, which is in serious trouble. The Fisher King, the king of the castle, has been wounded. His wounds are so severe that he cannot live, yet he is incapable of dying. He groans; he cries out; he suffers constantly. The whole land is in desolation, for a land mirrors the condition of its king, inwardly in a mythological dimension, as well as outwardly in the physical world. The cattle do not reproduce; the crops won't grow; knights are killed; children are orphaned; maidens weep; there is mourning everywhere—all because the Fisher King is wounded.

The notion that the welfare of a kingdom depends upon the virility or power of its ruler has been a common one, especially among primitive people. There are still kingdoms in the primitive parts of the world where the king is killed when he can no longer produce any offspring. He is simply killed, ceremonially, sometimes slowly, sometimes horribly, because it is thought that the kingdom will not prosper if the king is becoming weak.

The whole Grail castle is in serious trouble because the Fisher King is wounded. The myth tells us that years before, early in his adolescence, when he was out wandering around in the woods doing his knight errantry, the Fisher King came to a camp. All the people of the camp were gone, but there was a salmon roasting on a spit. He was hungry, there was the salmon roasting over the fire, and he took a bit of it to eat. He found that the salmon was very hot. After burning his fingers on it he dropped the salmon and put his fingers into his mouth to assuage the burn. In so doing he got a bit of the salmon into his mouth. This is the Fisher King wound and gives its name to the ruler of much of our modern psychology. Modern suffering man is the heir to this psychological event which took place culturally some eight hundred years ago.

Another version of the story has it that the young Fisher King was overwhelmed with *amour* one day and was out hunting for some experience of his passion. Another knight, a Muslim pagan, had had a vision of the True Cross and was out searching for some expression of this quest. The two came within sight of each other and, like true knights, each lowered visor and lance and went at the other. There was a terrible clash, the pagan knight was killed and the Fisher King received the wound in his thigh which blighted the kingdom for so many years.

What a sight! The knight of vision and the knight of sensuousness clash in terrible combat. Instinct and nature now suddenly having been touched by a vision of spirit clashing with pure spirit which has been touched by a vision of instinct and nature. Such is the crucible within which the highest evolution can take place—or a deadly conflict capable of psychological destruction.

I shudder at the implications of this clash, for it leaves us the legacy of our sensuous nature killed and our Christian vision terribly wounded. Hardly a modern man escapes this collision in his own life and he may end up in the sad state described in our story. His passion is killed and his vision is badly wounded.

The story of St. George and the dragon, which was adapted from a Persian myth at the time of the crusades, says much the same. In battle with the dragon, St. George, his horse, and the dragon were all mortally wounded. They would all have expired but for the fortuitous event that a bird pecked an orange (or a lime) that was hanging on a tree over St. George and a drop of the life-giving juice fell into his mouth. St. George arose, squeezed some of the elixir into his horse's mouth and revived him. No one revived the dragon.

3

Much is to be learned from the symbol of the wounded Fisher King. The salmon or, more generally, the fish, is one of the many symbols of Christ. As in the story of the Fisher King coming upon the roasting salmon, a boy in his early adolescence touches something of the Christ nature within himself but touches it too soon. He is unexpectedly wounded by it and drops it immediately as being too hot. But a bit of it gets into his mouth and he can never forget the experience. His first contact with what will be redemption for him later in his life is a wounding. This is what turns him into a wounded Fisher King. The first touch of consciousness in a youth appears as a wound or as suffering. Parsifal finds his Garden of Eden experience by way of the bit of salmon. That suffering stays with him until his redemption or enlightenment many years later.

Most western men are Fisher Kings. Every boy has naively blundered into something that is too big for him. He proceeds halfway through his masculine development and then drops it as being too hot. Often a certain bitterness arises, because, like the Fisher King, he can neither live with the new consciousness he has touched nor can he entirely drop it.

Every adolescent receives his Fisher King wound. He would never proceed into consciousness if it were not so. The church speaks of this wounding as the *felix culpa,* the happy fall which ushers one into the

4

process of redemption. This is the fall from the Garden of Eden, the graduation from naive consciousness into self consciousness.

It is painful to watch a young man realize that the world is not just joy and happiness, to watch the disintegration of his childlike beauty, faith, and optimism. It is regrettable but necessary—if we are not cast out of the Garden of Eden, there can be no Heavenly Jerusalem. In the Catholic liturgy for Holy Saturday evening there is a beautiful line, "Oh happy fall that was the occasion for so sublime a redemption."

The Fisher King wound may coincide with a specific event, an injustice, such as being accused of something we didn't do. In Dr. Jung's autobiography he tells that once his professor read all of Jung's classmate's papers in the order of their merit, but didn't read Jung's paper at all. His professor then said, "There is one paper here that is by far the best, but it is obviously a forgery. If I could find the book I would have him expelled." Jung had worked hard on the paper and it was his own creation. He never trusted that man, or the whole schooling process, after that. This was a Fisher King wound for Dr. Jung.

STAGES OF EVOLUTION

According to tradition, there are potentially three stages of psychological development for a man. The archetypal pattern is that one goes from the unconscious perfection of childhood, to the conscious imperfection of middle life, to conscious perfection of old age. One moves from an innocent wholeness, in which the inner world and the outer world are united, to a separation and differentiation between the inner and outer worlds with an accompanying sense of life's duality, and then, at last, to enlightenment—a conscious reconciliation of the inner and outer in harmonious wholeness.

ᔌ

We are witnessing the Fisher King's development from stage one to stage two. One has no right to talk about the last stage until he has accomplished the second one. One has no right to talk about the oneness of the universe until he is aware of its separateness and duality. We can do all manner of mental acrobatics and talk of the unity of the world; but we have no chance of functioning truly in this manner until we have succeeded in differentiating the inner and outer worlds. We have to leave the Garden of Eden before we can start the journey to the Heavenly

Jerusalem. It is ironic that the two are the same place but the journey must be made.

A man's first step out of the Garden of Eden into the world of duality is his Fisher King wound: the experience of alienation and suffering that ushers him into the beginning of consciousness. The myth tells us that the Fisher King wound is in the thigh. You may remember the biblical story about Jacob wrestling with the angel, he was wounded in the thigh. A touch of anything transpersonal—an angel or Christ in the guise of a fish—leaves the terrible wound that cries incessantly for redemption. The wound in the thigh means that the man is wounded in his generative ability, in his capacity for relationship. One version of the story has it that the Fisher King was wounded by an arrow that transfixed both testicles. The arrow could not be pushed through nor could it be withdrawn. Again, the Fisher King is described as being too ill to live but unable to die.

✍

Much of modern literature revolves around the lostness and alienation of the hero. Moreover, we can see this alienation in the countenance of almost everyone we pass on the street—the Fisher King wound is the hallmark of modern man.

I doubt if there is a woman in the world who has

not had to mutely stand by as she watched a man
agonize over his Fisher King aspect. She may be the
one who notices, even before the man himself is
aware of it, that there is suffering and a haunting
sense of injury and incompleteness in him. A man
suffering in this way is often driven to do idiotic
things to cure the wound and ease the desperation he
feels. Usually he seeks an unconscious solution outside of himself, complaining about his work, his
marriage, or his place in the world.

The Fisher King is carried about in his litter,
groaning, crying in his suffering. There is no respite
for him—except when he is fishing. This is to say
that the wound, which represents consciousness, is
bearable only when the wounded is doing his inner
work, proceeding with the task of consciousness
which was inadvertently started with the wound in
his youth. This close association with fishing will
soon play a large part in our story.

ᔥ

The Fisher King presides over his court in the Grail
castle where the Holy Grail, the chalice from the Last
Supper, is kept. Mythology teaches us that the king
who rules over our innermost court sets the tone and
character for that court and thus our whole life. If the
king is well, we are well; if things are right inside,

they will go well outside. With the wounded Fisher King presiding at the inner court of modern western man we can expect much outward suffering and alienation. And so it is: the kingdom is not flourishing; the crops are poor; maidens are bereaved; children are orphaned. This eloquent language expresses how a wounded archetypal underpinning manifests itself in problems in our external lives.

THE INNER FOOL

Every night there is a solemn ceremony in the Grail castle. The Fisher King is lying on his litter enduring his suffering while a procession of profound beauty takes place. A fair maiden brings in the lance which pierced the side of Christ at the crucifixion, another maiden brings the paten which held the bread at the Last Supper, another maiden brings the Grail itself which glows with light from its own depth. Each person is given wine from the Grail and realizes their deepest wish even before they voice that wish. Each person, that is, except the wounded Fisher King who may not drink from the Grail. This surely is the worst deprivation of all: to be barred from the essence of beauty and holiness when just those qualities are right in front of you is the cruelest of all suffering. All are served except the Grail king. All are conscious that their very center is deprived because their king can not partake of the grail.

I remember a time when beauty was denied me in just this manner. Many years ago I was particularly lonely and at odds with the world during a trip to visit my parents for Christmas. My journey took me through San Francisco and I stopped at my beloved Grace Cathedral. A performance of Handel's Messiah was scheduled for that evening so I stayed to hear this inspiring work. Nowhere is it better done than in that great building with its fine organ and master choristers. A few minutes into the performance I was so unhappy that I had to leave. It was then that I knew that the pursuit of beauty or happiness was in vain since I could not partake of the beauty even though it was immediately at hand. No worse or frightening pain is possible for us than to realize that our capacity for love or beauty or happiness is limited. No further outward effort is possible if our inward capacity is wounded. This is the Fisher King wound.

∽

How many times have women said to their men: "Look at all the good things you have; you have the best job you have ever had in your life. Our income is better than ever. We have two cars. We have two and sometimes three day weekends. Why aren't you happy? The Grail is at hand; why aren't you happy?"

The man is too inarticulate to reply, "Because I am a Fisher King and am wounded and cannot touch any of this happiness."

✍

A true myth teaches us the cure for the dilemma which it portrays. The Grail myth makes a profound statement of the nature of our present day ailment and then prescribes its cure in very strange terms.

The court fool (and every good court has its resident fool) had prophesied long ago that the Fisher King would be healed when a wholly innocent fool arrived in the court and asked a specific question. It is a shock to us that a fool should have to answer to our most painful wound but this solution is well known to tradition. Many legends put our cure in the hands of a fool or someone most unlikely to carry healing power.

The myth is telling us that it is the naive part of a man that will heal him and cure his Fisher King wound. It suggests that if a man is to be cured he must find something in himself about the same age and about the same mentality as he was when he was wounded. It also tells us why the Fisher King cannot heal himself, and why, when he goes fishing, his pain is eased though not cured. For a man to be truly healed he must allow something entirely different from himself to enter into his consciousness and change him. He cannot be healed if he remains in the old Fisher King mentality. That is why the young fool part of himself must enter his life if he is to be cured.

In my consulting room a man barks at me when I prescribe something strange or difficult for him: "What do you think I am? A Fool?" And I say, "Well, it would help." This is humbling medicine to accept.

A man must consent to look to a foolish, innocent, adolescent part of himself for his cure. The inner fool is the only one who can touch his Fisher King wound.

Parsifal

The story now turns from the Fisher King and his wound to the story of a boy who is of so little conse-quence that he has no name. He is born in Wales, during that time a country geographically on the fringe of the known world and a cultural backwater, the least likely place for a hero to appear and it reminds one of another Hero who was born in an unlikely place. What good could come out of Nazareth? Who would ever think of Wales as possi-bly producing an answer to our suffering? Myth in-forms us that our redemption will come from the least likely place. This reminds us again that it will be a humbling experience to find our redemption from the highly sophisticated wound of the Fisher King. The origin of the word 'humble' traces back to 'humus'—it means of the earth, feminine, unsophis-ticated. This reminds us of the biblical injunction,

"Except ye become as a little child, ye cannot enter the Kingdom of Heaven."

In his typology of the personality Dr. Jung observes that every educated person has one superior function of the four functions of feeling, thinking, sensing, and intuiting, which make up the human temperament. Also as a part of our psychology there is an opposing inferior function. While our superior function produces most of the high value of our life, the more developed personality strengths, it also leads us into our Fisher King wound. Our inferior function, that part of us which is least differentiated, will heal us from that wound. So it is the innocent fool from Wales who will heal the Fisher King.

The boy is of such lowly origin that he has no name when we first meet him; later we will learn that his name is Parsifal—innocent fool. The name also has a deeper meaning—he who draws the opposites together—and foretells his healing role, something like the meaning of the Chinese word, *tao*.

Dr. Jung describes an occasion when he was forced to rely on just this faculty in himself. The falling out between Jung and Freud occurred over the nature of the unconscious. Freud said that the unconscious is the repository of all the inferior elements of the personality, the unvalued things of one's life. Jung insisted that the unconscious is also the matrix, the artesian well from which all creativity springs. Freud would have none of this, so the two parted. That was a frightening experience for Dr. Jung since he was young and untried, with no reputation of his own. It looked as if he were finishing an abortive career before it began.

Dr. Jung knew where to look for the cure of his desperate wound and looked to his inner world. He locked himself in his room and waited on the unconscious. Soon he was down on the floor playing childish games. This led to the recall of his childhood fantasies which soon filled his attention. For months he labored daily in the privacy of his fantasy and in his backyard he built stone villages, towns and forts. He had fantasied all of this as a boy. He trusted his childlike experience and that was the beginning of an outpouring from the collective unconscious from which we have the legacy of Jungian psychology. A great man was humble (earthy) enough to trust his Parsifal for his cure.

Parsifal (we will call him that though he does not have a name until much later in the story) is raised by his mother, whose name is Heart's Sorrow. His father is dead and he knows nothing of him. He has no brothers or sisters. The redeeming hero in mythology often has no father and is raised in humble and lonely circumstances.

Parsifal grows up in primitive, peasant way, wears homespun clothes, has no schooling, asks no questions, and is completely untutored.

Early in his adolescence he is out playing one day when five knights came riding by wearing all their impressive equipment: the scarlet and gold trappings, the armor, the shields, the lances, all the accouterments of the knighthood. They dazzled poor Parsifal so completely that he dashed home to tell his mother he had seen five gods. He was on fire with this marvelous sight and decided to leave immediately to join the five wonderful men.

His mother burst into tears after seeing there was no way to stop her son from following in the footsteps of his father, who had been a knight and who was killed in some foolishness. His mother had tried to shield Parsifal from knowing anything of his lineage, but no mother has ever succeeded in keeping her son from danger when his father's blood begins to stir in him.

Heart's Sorrow (for this is the character of the moment as viewed by any mother) then tells Parsifal that his father had been a knight and been killed rescuing a fair maiden. His two brothers were knights and had also been killed. Heart's Sorrow had taken Parsifal to a remote place to raise him in hope he could be shielded from a similar fate.

Heart's Sorrow gives Parsifal her blessing and releases him from her protection. She can not resist giving him advice as he leaves: to respect fair damsels and instruction not to ask too many questions. Also he receives the gift of a single homespun garment she has woven for him. These are the legacies she bestows upon him. These two gifts will reverberate throughout the whole story and be instrumental in many of the complexities of what follows.

PARSIFAL'S JOURNEY

Parsifal goes off happily to find his five knights and begin his career as a man.

Parsifal asks everyone he meets, "Where are the five knights?" The look in an adolescent's eyes when he searches for his five knights is the question, "Where is it?"—the "it" always being only vaguely defined. A youth has had his first glimpse of meaning and value in the form of the five-ness of life and he searches throughout most of his adult life for experiences that will embody this quality. The number five implies the completion of life and is the root from which we form our word, *quintessence,* the fifth essence. Five implies completion. The five is everywhere, but elusively, also nowhere. It seems cruel to flash a vision of completion to a sixteen-year-old boy and set him on the road to find embodiment of that quality. But such is the motivation of any true spiritual life.

In his searching Parsifal comes to a tent. He never had seen a tent before, for he had grown up in a simple hut. The tent is the most magnificent place he has ever seen, so he presumes he has come to the divine cathedral of his mother's stories. He bursts into the tent to worship and finds a fair damsel. This is the first of a glittering, dazzling, incomprehensible array of fair damsels whom Parsifal will meet.

Parsifal remembers his mother's instructions to treat women fairly. He also remembers not to ask too many questions. He proceeds to cherish the fair maiden by embracing her and taking the ring from her finger as a talisman from her. This will be his inspiration for the rest of his life.

Have you ever seen a boy on his first date? He is always Parsifal blundering into the fair damsel's tent for the first time.

Parsifal had been told by his mother that he would have all the nourishment, all the food that he would need for his life in God's church, and it is all there before him in the form of a table set for a banquet. The damsel is waiting for her beloved knight, who is courting her, and she has spread out her best for him. But to Parsifal this is prophesy working out perfectly; here is God's temple, here is the fair damsel, here is everything he could wish to eat. Everything is just as his mother said it would be. Parsifal sits down to eat at the table and find that life is good.

The damsel by this time is becoming aware that she is in the presence of an extraordinary person. She is not angry for she sees that before her is a truly holy, simple, guileless person. She implores Parsifal to leave immediately because if her knight comes and finds him in the tent Parsifal will be killed.

Parsifal obeys the maiden and leaves her tent. He finds that life is good just as his mother had taught him.

THE RED KNIGHT

Parsifal asks everyone he finds how he may become a knight. He is informed that he should go to Arthur's Court where he will be knighted by the King if he is strong and brave enough.

He finds his way to Arthur's Court where he is laughed out of the great hall for his naivete, the look of his homespun garment, and his rashness at asking to be knighted. He is told that knighthood is an arduous life and that to be made a knight is an honor won only after much valor and noble work. Parsifal asks again and again until finally he is brought before King Arthur himself. Arthur, a kindly man, doesn't scorn Parsifal but tells him he must learn a great deal and be versed in all the knightly arts of battle and courtliness before he can be knighted.

Now there is in Arthur's Court a damsel who has not smiled nor laughed for six years. The legend in the Court is that when the best knight in the world appears, the damsel who has not smiled for six years will burst into laughter. The instant this damsel sees Parsifal, she bursts into laughter and joy. The Court is mightily impressed with this; apparently the best knight in the world has appeared! Here is this naive youth, this boy in a homespun garment, completely untutored, and the maiden is laughing. Extraordinary!

Until the Parsifal part of a man's nature appears, there is a feminine part of him that has never smiled, that is incapable of happiness, and she bursts into laughter and joy at the sight of Parsifal. If one can awaken the Parsifal in a man, another quality in him immediately becomes happy. When the court sees the doleful maiden laughing they treat Parsifal more seriously and King Arthur knights him then and there!

I had an experience of this recently. A man came to my office in tears, caught in the darkness of life. It was difficult to talk with him as he could see nothing but the dread of life. So I told him old tales and drew him into taking part in the stories. I drew out the Parsifal in him and found his childlike quality. Soon he was laughing and the maiden in him who hadn't known joy for six years burst forth. Then he had energy and courage to bring to his cheerless life. The awakening of Parsifal in a man constellates energy in him and he can function again.

Parsifal returns to Arthur and says, "I have a request. I want the horse and the armor of the Red Knight." Everyone laughs uproariously because there has not been a knight in King Arthur's Court strong enough to stand up to the Red Knight. Arthur too laughs and says, "You have my permission. You may have the horse and armor of the Red Knight—if you can get it."

As Parsifal leaves Arthur's court he is met at the door by the Red Knight. This wonderful being is strong enough to do as he wishes without fear, for no one in the court can oppose him. He had taken the silver cup, the Chalice, and no one was strong enough to stop him. As the last insult, he had thrown a flagon of wine in Queen Guenevere's face.

Parsifal is dazzled by the Red Knight with his red armor, his scarlet tunic, his horse's trappings, and all the stuff of knighthood. Parsifal stops the Red Knight and asks for his armor. The Red Knight is amused by the young fool before him and with a guffaw replies, "Fine, if you can get it."

The two square off, as knights are wont to do, and

have a brief battle in which Parsifal is knocked ig-
nominiously to the ground. But as he lies there he
throws his dagger at the Red Knight and kills him by
a wound in the eye. This is the only killing Parsifal
commits and represents a very important part in the
development of a young man. Esther Harding, in her
book *Psychic Energy,* discusses at length the evolution
of psychic energy from the stage of instinct to the
stage of ego-controlled energy. In moment that Parsifal kills the Red Knight, he relocates a very large
sum of energy from the Red Knight, that is, instinct,
to himself, as ego. One can say this is the moment
when he leaves adolescence and becomes a man. A
further development is required of him when he
again relocates this sum of energy from the ego to the
self or to that center of gravity which is greater than
any personal life. But that story is for later in the
myth.

Parsifal subdues many knights in his career but
none are killed. He extracts a promise from each
knight he conquers that he will go to the Court of
King Arthur and put himself in the service of that
noble King. This is the cultural process operating in
a man in the middle section of his life where he
conquers one center of energy after another and puts
them under the control of the Noble King. This is
truly the process of nobility in a man's life and is the
highest good for that middle section of his career.

No explanation is given for the killing of the Red Knight. It gives pause for thought if one examines what might have happened in our Western Culture if the Red Knight had been sent to serve at Arthur's Court rather than being killed. A study of the teachings of India give an alternative way of coping with the Red Knight energy in us. These teachings prescribe that one reduce the duality between Good and Evil in one's life—and thus reduce the power of the Red Knight—rather than kill that energetic quality and attach it to the ego. But our western way is to go the heroic path and to vanquish—by killing or conquering—and find victory in this way.

The victory over the Red Knight may happen outwardly or inwardly in a young man's life. The two ways are equally effective. If he is to follow an outer path, as most do, he must overcome some great obstacle. Many a Red Knight victory takes place on the playing field in competition or in some feat of endurance or in winning a victory of some other sort.

One of the bitter dimensions of life is that winning is generally at the cost of another's loss. Perhaps this is the Red Knight killing. Victory seems sweetest in the presence of another who has lost. This may be inherent in masculinity or it may be a phase of evolution which will one day be surmounted. At present, subduing the Red Knight is fierce and bloody.

There is an inner dimension possible for Red

Knighting; a boy may conquer a rough or rude sum of energy inside himself, overcome a bully or a clever cheat within. This is equally effective in making the transition from boy to man. This is native language to the introverts of our society.

If the Red Knight battle goes badly, either inwardly or outwardly, that sum of energy will go rampant in the personality and emerge as a bully, a vandal, or an angry young man. It can also take the form of the beaten and defeated shy man.

The Red Knight is the shadow side of masculinity, the negative, potentially destructive power. To truly become a man the shadow personality must be struggled with, but it cannot be repressed. The boy must not repress his aggressiveness since he needs the masculine power of his Red Knight shadow to make his way through the mature world.

Parsifal now owns the Red Knights armor and his horse, for in those days to conquer was to own. This is to say that the Red Knight energy is now under Parsifal's control and is his to use.

He tries to put on the Red Knight's wonderful armor but he has never before seen anything so complicated as a buckle and he can not manage the armor. A page who came out of Arthur's Court to see what the battle was about assists Parsifal in the mysteries of buckles and such complicated things of chivalry. The page urges Parsifal to take off his awful

one-piece homespun garment, which is unbefitting a
knight. But Parsifal refuses and clings to the one-
piece garment given to him by his mother. This is to
have serious repercussions later and it will take all
our powers of comprehension to see what is implied
in this clinging to the mother's garment. Parsifal puts
the armor on over his homespun garment and rides
away. What boy does not impose his newfound
knighthood over his mother complex? The stern
stuff of chivalry works very badly when it only cov-
ers a mother-complexed man. One more mystery
remains; though he can get his horse started, no one
has ever taught him how to stop it. He rides all day
until both horse and rider stop in sheer exhaustion.
Have you some memory of a project you began in
your early youth which started easily enough but
stopping it eluded you?

GOURNAMOND

Parsifal then discovers Gournamond, a godfather. A
godfather is such a boon to a boy at the time he is
turning into a man! One's own father has probably
worn out or the communication has grown thin
about the time a boy reaches adolescence. He is far
from independent but he is also too proud to go to
his father with intimate matters. It is a rare house-
hold today where intimacy still happens between

father and adolescent son. At this moment the boy needs a godfather, the man who will continue to train him after his father has lost contact with him. Gournamond is the archetypal godfather and spends a year training Parsifal in the ways of knighthood.

Gournamond teaches Parsifal information vital to attaining manhood; he must never seduce or be seduced by a fair maiden and he must search for the Grail castle with all his might. Specifically, he is to ask a certain question, "Whom does the Grail serve?" when he reaches the Grail castle. What would knighthood be worth if it were not for this noble end? Both of these instructions from Gournamond are worthy of discussion and will soon find their place in our narrative.

After these instructions Parsifal suddenly remembers his mother and goes in search of her again. Perhaps we can stand only so much of masculinity before we need to be in contact with feminine mother energy again.

So off he goes to hunt for his mother. He finds that soon after he left her, she died of a broken heart. You remember her name was Heart's Sorrow, which is part of motherhood. Naturally, Parsifal feels dreadfully guilty about his mother's death, but it is also part of his masculine development. No son ever develops into manhood without, in some way, being disloyal to his mother. If he remains with her, to comfort her and console her, then he never gets out of his mother complex. Often a mother will do all she can to keep her son with her. One of the most subtle ways is to encourage in him the idea of being loyal to her; but if he gives in to her completely then she often finds herself with a son severely injured in his masculinity. The son must ride off and leave his mother, even if it appears to mean disloyalty, and the mother must bear this pain. Later, like Parsifal, the son may come back to the mother and they may find a new relationship, on a new level; but this can only be done after the son has first achieved his independence and transferred his affection to a woman, either in an *interior* way with his own inner feminine side or in an *exterior* way with a real female companion of his own age. In our myth, Parsifal's mother died when he left. Perhaps she represents the kind of woman who can only exist as mother, who dies when this role is taken from her because she does not understand how to be an individual woman, but only a "mother."

BLANCHE FLEUR

Many people set forth on their journeys through life in good faith but with very little psychological understanding of why they are going on that particular journey or of where it might take them. Sometimes they do have an intended goal but fail to achieve that goal. Often fate will serve them unexpectedly and a far deeper purpose may be accomplished. So it is with Parsifal's search for his mother. He finds, instead, Blanche Fleur—which means "White Flower"—and comes into awareness of the highest motivation of his life before the grail encounter.

Blanche Fleur is in distress and her castle is under siege. She implores Parsifal to rescue her kingdom. Obeying that profound law, "A man knows not his strength until it is needed," he frees her domain of the intruders. He does this by searching out the second in command of the besieging army, duelling heroically with him, sparing his life at the last moment, and sending him in fealty to the court of King Arthur. He repeats this with the first in command. We are seeing the first of a long series of encounters that will add to the fellowship of the round table.

This is a poetic way of describing the process Dr. Jung speaks of as "relocating the center of gravity of the personality," a careful and highly conscious process of drawing from the untamed pool of masculine energy and adding to the conscious center of the personality, which is here represented by King Arthur and his round table. No endeavor is more noble or heroic than this ideal in the first half of one's life.

It is in the service of Blanche Fleur that Parsifal

performs his heroic task; she is his lady fair and the carrier of inspiration, the very core of heroic action, for everything Parsifal accomplishes. It is not by accident that it was the mother-search which led the blundering Parsifal to she-who-will-inspire, truly the animating principle of life. It is a moment of poetic beauty to find what Dr. Jung called this inspirer in a man's bosom, the Anima, she who animates and is the fountain of life in the heart of man. Blanche Fleur, indeed, deserves her name.

Her conduct in the rest of the story would be bitterly disappointing if one were to consider her a flesh-and-blood woman; for all she does is remain in her castle as a symbol of inspiration or perhaps a talisman of affection—when Parsifal occasionally comes dashing back for a moment of her beauty and trust. But taken as that interior feminine, deep in the heart of a man, she is the very core of inspiration and meaning. A rose from her hand or a glance of approval is sufficient to provide motive and strength for the most heroic of deeds. Though this is couched in medieval terms and is encased in the stuff of chivalry, it is no less present in the most modern of men.

After raising the siege from her castle, Parsifal returns to spend one night with Blanche Fleur. We are given a detailed account of how they slept together in the most intimate embrace—head to head, shoulder to shoulder, hip to hip, knee to knee, toe to toe.

But the embrace was chaste and worthy of the knight's vow that he never seduce or be seduced by a fair maiden; a vow he must keep if he is to win a vision of the Grail.

Many inner truths are shorn of their true power by being transposed to a level inconsistent with their power and depth. Viewing the virgin birth of Christ as only a historical event will blur the sight of a vital law which is needed when you are called upon to make that interior mating of the human soul with the Divine Spirit which is the true genesis of one's individuality.

Much of our religious heritage is a map or set of instructions for the deepest meaning of our interior life, not a set of laws for outer conduct. To relate to our religious teaching only in its literal dimension is to lose its spiritual meaning. This dimension of materialism is far more harmful than much of what is usually condemned under that dark name.

Chastity

Gournamond's instruction—never to seduce a fair maiden or be seduced by her—is of such profound importance to our story that it is worthy of a chapter in its own right.

It is important to remember that we are studying a myth much as one would study a dream, and many of the same laws apply. A dream is almost entirely an inner matter and every part of a dream is to be construed as part of the dreamer. Example: if a man dreams of a fair damsel; it is almost certain that his own feminine inner capacity is being addressed. It is only too easy to literalize such a dream figure and explain it as one's sexual interest or a comment on one's current girlfriend. If one makes this error the true depth of the dream will be lost.[1] So also in myth;

---

[1] See Robert A. Johnson, *Inner Work: Using Dreams and Active Imagination for Personal Growth* (San Francisco: Harper & Row, Publishers, Inc., 1986), for a further elaboration of this principle.

if we take Gournamond's instruction in a literal sense, we will have little but a caricature of medieval chivalry before us.

What is this inner femininity which Parsifal is to stay aloof from? It is all the softness of femininity that is so valuable in an inner sense but that would vitiate him if he mistook it and lived it in an outer sense.

MOOD AND FEELING

Feeling is the ability to value: mood is being over-taken or possessed by the inner feminine. To feel is the sublime art of having a value structure and a sense of meaning—where one belongs, where one's allegiance is, where one's roots are. To mood (we are already in difficulty since there is no adequate term for being caught up in a mood) is to be in the grips of the feminine part of our nature, to be over-whelmed by an irrational element that plays havoc with a man's outer life. The feminine side of a man is to connect him within the depths of his inner being and to make a bridge to his deepest self.[2]

[2]Mood, strictly speaking, should be confined to describing a man's experi-ence since the parallel phenomenon in a woman is sufficiently different to require a different term. But no term exists for this and we have no adequate language to describe this parallel experience in a woman's life. In this con-text a woman's parallel to male moods is being delivered over to her inner masculine side and thus subject to a sharpness, a puncturing, a challenging,

Often a man has to make a choice between feeling and mood. If he is engaging in one of these, there is no room for the other. A mood prohibits true feeling, even though a mood may appear to be feeling. If a man is engaging in a mood—or, more accurately, when a mood has engaged him—he automatically forfeits the ability for true feeling and thus for relationship and creativity. In the old language he has seduced or been seduced by his interior femininity. A man never wears femininity outwardly with any validity. A man overwhelmed by a mood is a sundial in moonlight telling the wrong time. His interior femininity serves him well as "la femme inspiritrice" when she is rightly placed; but she does not serve him well when he wears her as an outer garment and uses her to relate to his outer world. "Uses" is the pertinent word here; anyone and everything around a man feels "used" when he relates to the world by way of a mood. Seduction, indeed! Feeling, on the contrary, is a sublime part of a man's equipment and brings warmth, gentleness, relatedness, and perception.

We often project our relationship, or lack of one,

---

a needling quality which is a type of poor quality masculinity. This is similar to a man's mood, which is a type of poor quality femininity. For a more adequate discussion of the subject see Robert A. Johnson, *She: Understanding Feminine Psychology*, Revised Edition (New York: Harper & Row Publishers, Inc., 1989).

with our inner femininity onto an outer flesh-and-blood woman. Human woman is a miracle in her own right, a beauty which will be obscured if we try to put the laws of inner woman upon her. So, too, is inner woman clouded if we treat her in an outer way.[3]

Man has only two alternatives for relationship to his inner woman: either he rejects her and she turns against him in the form of bad moods and undermining seductions, or he accepts her and finds within a companion who walks through life with him giving him warmth and strength. If a man falls under the spell of a mood, that is, if he misconstrues her as being "out there," he loses his capacity for relationship. This is true even though it might be a "good mood" or a "bad" one.

Creativity in a man is directly linked with his inner feminine capacity for growth and creation. Genius in a man is his interior feminine capacity to give birth; it is his masculinity which gives him capacity for putting that creativity into form and structure in the outer world.

Goethe, in his masterpiece, *Faust,* came to the noble conclusion late in his life that it is the province of man to serve woman. He ends *Faust* with the lines

[3]See Robert A. Johnson, *We: Understanding the Psychology of Romantic Love,* (San Francisco: Harper & Row Publishers, Inc., 1983), for further discussion of this subject.

"The Eternal Feminine draws us onward"—certainly a reference to the inner woman. To serve the Grail is to serve the inner woman.

An alert woman knows the instant a man in her life succumbs to a mood for all relating stops that very instant. A glazed look comes over the eyes of the man and the woman knows he has abdicated from any relationship. Even a good mood costs one relationship. All ability to relate, objectivity and creativity, come to an end when mood takes control. In Hindu terminology, serving the goddess Maya (the equivalent of our anima moods) costs one all reality and substitutes a vaporous unreality in its place. Myth often overstates its case in its timeless language, and one's chance for a vision of the Grail is not lost forever. But so long as the mood is dominant there is no Grail: the mood imprints its character on the objective world and all objective vision of the true splendor of the world is lost. One literally sells one's birthright for a mess of illusion.

The worst characteristic of mood possession is that it robs one of all sense of meaning. Suddenly the "out there" is dominant in one's inner life and the inner meaning of life is lost. One is then at the mercy of the "out there" for one's sense of value or happiness. One is so tied to a new purchase or gaining the favor of someone that he is unaware of his own inner meaning, which is the only stable value he has.

Mood possession also robs him of the objective world and its true beauty and magnificence, a deep meaning in its own right.

DEPRESSION AND INFLATION

Depression and inflation are other names for mood. Both give one a sense of being overwhelmed by something other than one's true self. This is weakness and incompetence in a man.

Moods turn one to outer things or people for one's sense of value and meaning. What American garage is not piled high with things that a man bought hoping they would bring him a sense of meaning—only to be discarded when they failed to bring whatever he longed for? Material things are valid in their own right and bring high value when related to properly; but when one asks them to carry an inner value they fail miserably. The one exception to this law is when some physical object carries an inner value that is meaningful as a symbol or in a ceremony. A gift from a friend can symbolize the high value between two people if it is consciously invested with this value. It will fail him and add to the collection in the garage if he asks it to carry that value aside from symbol or ceremony.

No thing in itself is either good or bad; a man may take out his fishing gear one Saturday and have a wonderful and relaxing time fishing. The next Saturday he may have a bad anima attack and come home from fishing in a terrible mood. It is the level of consciousness that determines the difference between these two experiences. Outer value and inner value are both profoundly real; it is only when they are mixed or contaminated with each other that they can cause trouble.

A man is not master in his own interior house when he is in a mood. A usurper has taken first place and the man's response will be to fight the usurper. Unfortunately, he often chooses to fight this battle on the wrong level—in other words he will fight with his wife or his environment instead of facing the battle within, which would be the only appropriate action. Mythology describes the hero's battle with his internal self as the encounter with the dragon, and modern man has no fewer dragon battles than did his medieval counterpart. You can update mythology and make it dramatically alive if you can find the modern stage on which the dragon battles, even fair maidens and red knights will play out their drama.

HAPPINESS

Good moods are no less dangerous than the dark ones. To demand happiness from one's environment is the dark art of seducing the interior fair maiden. This obscures the Grail no less than being seduced by fair maiden, though it is less obvious.

Here is a differentiation easy to miss: that exuberant, top-of-the-world, bubbling, half-out-of-control mood so highly prized among men is also mood possession and is as dangerous as the dark mood. In a dark mood a man has seduced his anima and has her by the throat saying, "You are going to make me happy—or else!" This is to draw her into the lesser affairs of the ego's demands for happiness or one's restless quest for entertainment.

✺

To be caught by an exuberant mood is also to be seduced by the inner woman. She wafts him off to dizzy heights of inflation and gives him a wonderful facsimile of the happiness he legitimately wants. Such a seduction exacts a high price later in the form of a depression that brings the man down to earth again. Fate spends much time bringing a man up from his depression or down from his inflation. It is this ground level which the ancient Chinese called the *tao*, the middle way. It is here that the Grail exists and happiness worthy of the name can be found. This is not a kind of gray average place or a place of compromise but is the place of true color, meaning, and happiness. It is nothing less than Reality, our true home.

One form of seduction is to wring pleasure from an experience in advance. I know two young fellows who planned a camping trip. In their glory, for days ahead of the trip, they planned how great it was going to be. All the mood characteristics arose. Bits of equipment suddenly became Holy Grails: they marveled at the sharpness of this knife or the efficiency of that bit of rope. These fellows milked all the happiness out of that experience far in advance. Later I found that they went to the anticipated place, kicked around for half a day, couldn't think of anything to do, got into the car and came home the same day—there was nothing there. They had seduced the life out of the experience in advance.

Modern western man has some basic misconceptions about the nature of happiness. The origin of the word is instructive: *happiness* stems from the root verb *to happen,* which implies that our happiness is what happens. Simple people in less complicated parts of the world function in this manner and exhibit a happiness and tranquility that is a puzzle to us. How can a peasant in India with so little to be happy about be so happy? Or how can the peon in Mexico, again with so little to be happy about, be as carefree as he appears? These people know the art of *happiness,* contentment with what is. Their happiness is what happens. If you can not be happy at the prospect of lunch it is not likely you will be happy over anything.

A Hindu sage taught that the highest form of worship was simply to be happy. But this was happy in its profound sense, not a mood.

Thomas Merton, the Trappist monk, once said that a monk may often be happy but he never has a good time. This is another way of differentiating happiness from mood.

For many years of my life I thought one came down with a mood just as one comes down with a cold. But slowly I learned that moods are a product of purposeful unconsciousness and can be rectified by the very consciousness one worked so hard to evade.

One can contrast mood with enthusiasm. The latter is one of the most beautiful words in our vocabulary. It means "to be filled with God," *en-theo-ism.* It is a highly rewarding and valid experience to touch an enthusiasm. At the very opposite end of the scale it is painful to be possessed by a mood. When you laugh it is a divine act if you are filled with the joy of God; but it is blasphemy if you are swept off your feet by a mood. Happiness is entirely legitimate; mood invites the ensuing depression.

A woman faces a delicate challenge when her man

has fallen into a mood. If she brings forth her parallel to it and begins needling him she sets off a highly negative exchange. Yet, a point of genius is possible for her in this situation; if she can be more feminine than the man's mood, react out of her deepest femininity—as contrasted with his misplaced femininity—this will give the man a vantage point of reality from which he can move out of his poor quality mood. It is a severe temptation to a woman to needle or puncture; but her own natural femininity is never more creative than when it can be an anchor for a man caught in the whirlwind of his interior femininity. This requires a conscious and well-developed femininity in a woman. It is the result of the many dragon battles she must fight to safeguard her own inner feminine kingdom.[4]

A woman must also understand that a man is much less in control or aware of things feminine than she is. Many women presume that a man should be as able as she to control the ever-shifting play of light and dark, angel and witch in the feminine element. No man is capable of the same kind of control as she has, and if a woman understands this she can be patient and understanding as the man bungles along some light years behind her in his feminine

[4]How badly we flounder for terminology to express these things. Where is our word for queendom?

understanding. The reverse is true in some other departments of life.

In our myth Parsifal and Blanche Fleur make a perfect example of the correct relationship of man and inner woman. They are close to each other, each warms the other and makes life meaningful for the other; but there is no seduction. This is a sublime definition of man and inner woman; but if it were taken as example of man and flesh-and-blood woman it would be a ridiculous boy scout story. This misconstruing of levels has caused havoc with those following the medieval instructions of the way-of-the-knight. Inner relationships have their own inexorable laws of conduct; outer relationships have their own equally explicit laws. Do not mix the two.

The Grail Castle

Our story goes on.

Parsifal has traveled all day in his heroic quest and at nightfall asks someone if there is a lodge or tavern anywhere nearby where he can spend the night. He is informed that there is no habitation within thirty miles.

A little later Parsifal finds a man in a boat fishing on a lake. He asks the man if there is any place to stay the night. The fisherman, who is the Fisher King, invites him to his humble abode, "Just go down the road a little way, turn left, cross the drawbridge." Parsifal does this and the drawbridge snaps shut just as he crosses it and ticks the back hooves of his horse. It is very dangerous to enter into the Grail castle, for that is the Fisher King's home, and many a youth is unhorsed as he makes the transition from our ordinary world into the imaginary, symbolic world of the Grail castle.

Parsifal finds himself in the keep of a great castle where four youths take his horse, bath him, give him fresh clothing, and lead him to the master of the castle, the Fisher King. The King apologizes for being unable to rise from his litter and greet Parsifal properly due to his wound. The whole court of the castle—four hundred knights and ladies—is there to greet Parsifal, and a wonderful ceremony takes place.

In a setting of such grandeur one knows that Parsifal has blundered into the inner world, the place of the spirit, the place of transformation. Especially when the number four is accentuated—four hundred knights and ladies, four youths, the great fireplace with four faces showing the cardinal directions—one expects the splendor of the inner world. It is indeed the Grail castle where the Holy Grail from the last supper is kept.

There is a great ceremony in progress. The Fisher King lies groaning in agony on his litter, one fair maiden carries in the lance that pierced the side of Christ, another fair maiden brings the paten from which the last supper was served, and, finally, a third fair maiden brings in the Holy Grail itself.[5]

A great banquet is held and everyone is given what they wish from the Grail or the paten even before they formulate a wish. Everyone, that is, except the Fisher King. Because of his wound he is unable to drink from the Grail, and his suffering is the worse because of this deprivation.

The Fisher King's niece brings a sword which the King straps to Parsifal's waist. This sword is to be Parsifal's for the rest of his life. It is here that a youth gains his mature masculinity and his power to accomplish the remaining tasks of his life.

Another gift is available at the Grail castle but Parsifal does not pass the test required for this. Gournamond instructed Parsifal during his training that when he found the Grail he was to ask a specific question, "Whom does the Grail serve?" If this question is asked the blessings of that great cornucopia of life, the Grail, will pour out its blessings. Without the question one may drink from the Grail but its great bounty will not flow out. Though Gournamond had instructed him in this question, Parsifal's mother had told him when he was leaving her not to ask too

[5]Here is a correct place for the interior woman in a man's psychology; it is she who is mediator for him to the numinous values of the inner world.

45

many questions, sound advice to a querulous youth, but nearly fatal here. His mother's advice prevails and Parsifal stands mute before all the splendor of the Grail castle. It is understandable that a sixteen-year-old country youth would not find the strength or courage to ask the most important question of life at such a moment. To ask would require that he be conscious.

More than this, and of deeper significance, there was a legend in the Grail castle that one day an innocent fool would wander into the castle, ask the Grail question, and thus heal the wounded Fisher King. Everyone in the castle—except Parsifal—knows this legend and watches keenly to see if Parsifal, who has all the attributes of an innocent fool, will ask the healing question.

But Parsifal does not ask and the Fisher King is soon taken, groaning and writhing in agony, to his chamber. The other knights and ladies disperse and Parsifal is soon escorted to his sleeping chamber by the four youths.

Next morning Parsifal awakes to find himself alone. He saddles his horse and crosses the drawbridge, which snaps shut, ticking the back hooves of his horse (again a dangerous transition), and is back in the ordinary world. There is no castle to be seen and the innocent fool is again in the realm where "there is no habitation for thirty miles."

THE GRAIL CASTLE LOST

The most important event of one's inner life is portrayed in the story of the Grail castle. Every youth blunders his way into the Grail castle sometime around age fifteen or sixteen and has a vision that shapes much of the rest of his life. Like Parsifal, he is unprepared for this and does not have the possession to ask the question that would make the experience conscious and stable within him. No youth could be expected to do anything but wander into the castle, be overwhelmed by it, and the next morning find himself back in the same ordinary world—if he has not been unhorsed by the drawbridge.

Most men can remember a magic half hour sometime in their youth when the whole world glowed and showed a beauty not easily described. Perhaps it is a sunrise, a glorious moment on the playing field, a solitary time during a hike when one turns a corner and the whole splendor of the inner world opens for one. No youth can cope with this opening of the Heavens for him and most set it aside but do not forget it. Others find it so disturbing that they dismiss it and play as if it had never happened. A few are so touched by the vision of meaning that they spend the rest of their lives, like Parsifal, searching for the Grail castle again. One has only to "go down the road, turn left, cross the drawbridge." But the

47

very simplicity of the directions effectively hides it from view. How many times have we gone back to a magic place to see if the sunrise would glow again or set off for a reputedly magic place to see if the Grail procession is there? The imprint of the Grail castle is indelible in a man's mind, and if it is strong in him it will inspire or haunt him for the rest of his life.

Why was Parsifal not able to ask the simple question that would have opened a glorious world for him and healed the agony of the Fisher King's wound? He had been instructed to ask the question and it seems an act of stupidity that he fails it. Not so; naivete prevented him from asking.

THE MOTHER COMPLEX

Do you remember the one-piece homespun garment Parsifal's mother made for him? It is this remnant, under his knight's armor, which prevents him from appreciating the Grail when he sees it. So long as a man is encased in his mother complex he can not appreciate the Grail or, worse yet, ask the right question to heal the Fisher King wound. To get the mother's homespun off a youth is an arduous task. Many never succeed in divesting themselves from their mother complex, for that is what is symbolized by the mother's homespun. To examine this critical issue we must digress and talk about a man's relationship to things feminine.

There are six basic relationships a man bears to the feminine world. All six are useful to him and each has its own nobility. It is only the contamination of one with another that makes difficulty. These difficulties are central to a man's passage through life. The six feminine elements in a man are:

- His human mother. This is the actual woman who was his mother, she with all her idiosyncrasies, individual characteristics, and uniqueness.

- His mother complex. This resides entirely inside the man himself. This is his regressive capacity which would like to return to a dependency on his mother and be a child again. This is a man's wish to fail, his defeatist capacity, his subterranean fascination with death or accident, his demand to be taken care of. This is pure poison in a man's psychology.

- His mother archetype. If the mother complex is pure poison, the mother archetype is pure gold. It is the feminine half of God, the cornucopia of the universe, mother nature, the bounty which is freely poured out to us without fail.

We could not live for one minute without the bounty of the mother archetype. It is always reliable, nourishing, sustaining.

- His fair maiden. This is the feminine component in every man's psychic structure and is the interior companion or inspirer of his life, the fair damsel. It is Blanche Fleur, one's lady fair, Dulcinea in *Don Quixote*, Beatrice to Dante in the *Comedia Divina*. It is she who gives meaning and color to one's life. Dr. Jung named this quality the *anima*, she who animates and brings life.

- His wife or partner. This is the flesh and blood companion who shares his life journey and is a human companion.

- Sophia. This is the Goddess of Wisdom, the feminine half of God, the Shekinah in Jewish mysticism. It comes as a shock to a man to discover that Wisdom is feminine, but all mythologies have portrayed it so.

All of these feminine qualities are useful to man, even the mother complex, which is the most difficult. Faust had to rely on his mother complex to take him to the place of the mothers for his final redemption in Goethe's masterpiece. It is only in the mixing or contamination of one aspect with another that causes such profound distress. Mankind has a terrible propensity for making such muddles. Let us look at some of these contaminations and see the destruction which follows.

If one contaminates one's human mother with one's mother complex he will blame his actual mother for the regressive quality that is his interior mother complex: he will see his mother as a witch who is trying to defeat him. It is commonplace for a young man to blame his mother, or mother substitute, for his own regressive mother complex.

If he contaminates his interior mother image with the mother archetype he will expect his flesh and blood mother to play the goddess of protection for him, a role which only the archetype can provide. He will make ridiculously excessive demands on the mother aspect of the world and demand of the world that it owes him a living—preferably without effort on his part.

If one contaminates his anima, or fair maiden, with his interior mother image he will expect his inner woman to be mother to him.

A very common contamination is the overlay of mother and wife. Such a man will expect his wife to mother him instead of being a companion for him. He will demand of his wife that she fulfill his mother-expectations for him.

Since Sophia is not strong in every man's life this component is not always present. If a man confuses mother and Sophia he will endow his mother with Goddess-like wisdom that no human could ever sustain. "Mother knows best" and the Sophia archetype make a bad combination.

I leave the other combinations or contaminations to your own inquiry. They are all negative. It is not the feminine which is negative but only the contamination of levels of consciousness.

∿

To return to Parsifal and the question of why he failed at the Grail castle—it was the failure to remove his mother's homespun garment, his mother complex, which cost him the power and clarity to ask the question Gournamand had taught him. No man can relate to the Grail in a permanent way if his mother complex intervenes between him and his native masculine strength. It is to take twenty years of arduous knight-errantry to get Parsifal's homespun garment removed so that he can be the strong male who can stand the beauty of the Grail—the greatest symbol of the mother archetype. So long as one is clothed in mother's homespun, he can not partake of the Grail other than in an occasional chance encounter. Nor can he heal his Fisher King wound. The remaining years of adventure Parsifal experiences are all moving toward the removal of that homespun. One has a chance again at the Grail castle in middle age. The Grail is always near one and available at any moment but sixteen and forty-five, times of change, seem to be the two points in a man's life when it is most easily found. That miraculous procession goes on every night of one's life in the Grail castle; but it is only at particular times in his life—and then only when he has prepared for it—that a man has easy access to the splendor of the Grail castle.

Theoretically it should be possible for a man to stay in the Grail castle the first time. The Benedictine monks in medieval Europe observed this possibility in a monastic practice. They took boys at birth, raised them in the Grail castle and never let them out, psychologically speaking. They were never subjected to the pressures of the world, to courtship or marriage or to any possession or power structure in a worldly sense. I have never known anyone who had this experience, and I don't think it is possible for a modern person. Possibly such a way is open to a medieval mentality or a person of that character today.

A monastic sect in India tries another way of securing the Grail castle. They keep boys from birth to age sixteen in monastic seclusion, marry them at sixteen, and return them to monastic seclusion for the rest of their lives after their first child is born. In this way the space between the two Grail castles is only one year, instead of the usual thirty years that separate those encounters at sixteen and forty-five. Again, this may be possible for very simple medieval personalities but it is not available to us. (And one wonders about the wife and the child!)

If the Grail castle experience is very strong for a boy it nearly incapacitates him. The youth who wanders about seemingly without any motive or goal is often a young man who has been half-blinded by his Grail castle experience.

Many men find the whole experience of Grail castles so painful, so incomprehensible, that they immediately repress it and say, "I don't remember." Like all repressed things in the unconscious, far from having gotten rid of it, we find it is everywhere, behind every tree and around every corner, looking over the shoulder of every person we meet. The hunger for "something," the Saturday night restlessness, the tires squealing around the corner are all not-so-distant echoes of the Grail-castle hunger. The quest comes in many languages.

So much of a youth's bantam rooster behavior is a turning off of the Grail castle experience. It hurts so much he can't stand it and tries to persuade himself he is very tough in order to get away from the pain.

Much of advertising plays upon this hunger. I am not sure how consciously advertising specialists do this but they have an uncanny way of searching out this hunger in us. You can sell a man almost anything if you indirectly call it the Grail.

This is also the chief appeal and thrill of drugs. That is a magical way of getting back to the Grail ecstasy. Drugs will take you to an ecstatic experience and bring a legitimate visionary world; but they do it in a wrong way and exact a terrible price. The right way does not necessarily require a long time or a long way; but there are no shortcuts. If one cheats at the process, the drawbridge can snap shut at the wrong moment and one is trapped in a madness or hellish suffering.

If one thinks that something or somebody will fill the Grail hunger in him, no cost is too high. Much of the motivation of late adolescence—the derring-do, the ninety-miles-an-hour down the highway, the drugs—this is Grail hunger.

If the Grail quest is sidetracked by any of the many ways possible, the youth finds himself all too soon a crotchety old man.

I asked a friend once how he was. He replied very honestly, "Well, Robert, I am turning the crank." The Grail is far away at such a moment.

A woman experiences the Grail in quite a different way from a man. She never leaves the Grail castle and keeps a sense of beauty, connectedness, at-homeness in the universe that a man does not have.

A man creates out of his restlessness; a woman creates by knowing what always was. Parsifal had to go out to nearly endless knight adventures; Blanche Fleur stayed in her castle.

Einstein in his old age said, "I now bask in that solitude which was so painful to me in my youth." This is the Grail castle restored. He earned it by a lifetime of modern knight heroism.

Many men try to make a flesh and blood woman fill the Grail hunger. This is to ask a woman to fulfill a role she can never carry (who can be a living archetype?) and to miss the human miracle she is in fact.

The current fascination with Asian religions is a direct Grail quest. The Asia never fractured as we westerners did, and they never divided the secular and sacred worlds so tragically as we did. No traditional Asian ever strays far from the Grail castle. Asian teachers look at us and say, "What in the world is this great hurry and hunger in you people?" Someone spoke of us as "those aryan birds of prey." A people in the grips of so urgent a quest are indeed formidable.

The drawbridge is a hint about the nature of the Grail castle. It doesn't exist in physical reality. It is an inner reality, a vision, poetry, a mystical experience, and it can not be found in any outer place. To search for it outwardly is to exhaust one's self and to court discouragement. Still, our devotion to outer things as the only reality is so strong that for most of us it requires an outer exploration or drama to fuel the inner search. Even that is suspect, for the Grail is always immediately at hand and is won more by peeling away the insulations around it than by any act of creation. A medieval Christian proverb says, "To search for God is to insult God." This implies that God is always present and any search for him is a refusal of this fact. A surgeon friend of mine likes to say, "Don't fix what isn't broken." It is only an extension of that to say, "Don't search for that which is already at hand." But we are westerners and have to search in order to learn that there is no search.

A Chinese story has it: a fish heard some men talking on a pier about a miraculous substance called water. The fish was so intrigued that he called his fish friends together and profoundly announced he was going in quest of this wonderful stuff. They gave him a fitting ceremony and sent him on his way. Long after they had given him up as lost on his perilous journey he swam home, old, tired, worn. They hastened to greet him and asked urgently, "Did you find it? Did you find it?" "Yes," replied the old fish, "but you would not believe what I found." Whereupon the old fish swam slowly away.

There are highly instructive parallels between Christ's and Parsifal's journey. The two stories resemble each other in many ways, with the important difference that the very wise man, Christ, makes the quest in the right way. But he still had to go through all the stages. When Christ went to the temple at age twelve and rebuked his parents, this was his first Grail castle. He touched something very deep—his manhood, his strength. He wasn't badly wounded by it because he understood. He later had to go back to the Grail castle a second time to take up permanent residence there. He did all this in a very wise way, leaving a prototype for us to follow. I am fond of the old twelfth century Grail myth because it offers a more earthy and human statement of our path. I can find more of Parsifal in myself than I can of the martyr.

The Dry Years

Parsifal has left the grail castle and now must earn the right to return to it. He is involved in a long series of knight's ventures that gradually strengthen him sufficiently so he can ask for a second entrance to the Grail castle.

He comes upon a sorrowful maiden holding her dead lover in her arms. She explains tearfully that her knight-lover was killed by another knight in a rage over something Parsifal had done in one of his earlier naive escapades. Parsifal has to bear the guilt of this. The maiden asks Parsifal where he has been and when he tells her, she rebukes him saying there is no habitation within thirty miles. He describes his experiences in detail and she replies, "Oh, you have been in the Grail castle!" Women often know more of such experiences than men. Then she berates him for not asking the question and healing the Fisher King. This is also his fault. More guilt accumulates. She asks Parsifal his name. Though we have been using his name, Parsifal, the word has not actually appeared in the text until this moment. "Parsifal, he blurts out." Not until one has been in the Grail castle does he have a name, any sense of his own identity.

∽

Parsifal goes on to another weeping damsel who has also suffered much through some naive mischance from his earlier travels. This damsel informs Parsifal that his sword will break the first time he uses it and that it can be mended only by him who forged it originally. Once repaired, it will never break again.

This is a fine bit of advice for a youth; the masculine equipment he carries with him, largely imitation of the father-teachers around him, will not hold up when he tries to use it by himself. Every youth has to go through the humiliation of finding that his imitation masculinity will not hold up. And more, only the father who gave him his sword can repair the broken instrument. This means that what was given by a father can be repaired only by a father. A Godfather is a very valuable ally just at this moment. To have a Godfather who will repair what was transmitted from the father but did not hold up well is an extremely valuable asset.

Parsifal conquers many knights, sends them back to Arthur's court, rescues many fair damsels, lifts sieges, protects the poor, slays dragons—all the good things a man must do in the middle section of his life. This is the cultural process of making our civilization work. We smile at the stories of dragons and spells on castles but we suffer these things in our own times as directly as did any medieval man. We call them complexes or moods or shadow invasions now, but I find the old language at least (perhaps more) as descriptive as our own.

Parsifal's fame has come back to Arthur's court and the King sets out to find this great hero in his land. Parsifal is the greatest knight in the world, just as the maiden who had not laughed for seven years indicated. Arthur vows not to sleep two nights in the same bed until he has found this wonderful hero, the flower of his realm.

A curious experience comes to Parsifal just at this moment. He is wandering about on his knight's journey when a falcon attacks three geese in the air. Three drops of blood from one of them falls onto the snow near Parsifal and he drifts into a lover's trance at the sight. He is transfixed by the three drops of blood and can think of nothing but Blanche Fleur. King Arthur's men find him in this immobile state and two of them try to lead him to Arthur's court. He fights them off, breaking the arm of one; he is the knight who had jeered when the maiden laughed in Arthur's court. Parsifal had vowed to avenge her for this scorn. This vow is now completed.

Gawain, a third knight, asks Parsifal gently and humbly if he will come to Arthur's court and Parsifal agrees.

In another version of the story, the sun melts the snow and obliterates two of the drops of blood relieving Parsifal of the spell so that he can function again. It is possible that Parsifal would still be there in his lover's trance if the sun had not reduced the three drops of blood to one or if Gawain had not rescued him.

Curious symbolism is at work in this part of the story. When dreams or myth make much point of numbers it is certain that very deep parts of the collective unconscious are at work. Do you remember the great emphasis on four in the Grail castle? Here it is the number three which is highly accentuated. Four seems to be the language of the collective unconscious for peace, wholeness, completion, tranquility. Three is the symbol for urgency, incompleteness, restlessness, striving, accomplishment. Parsifal, having been profoundly touched by the fourness of the Grail castle now must cope with the threeness of here-and-now life. His loves, the knightly quest, his place in Arthur's court—these here-and-now things claim him. No one can make his way back to the Grail castle until he has made his way through the human dimensions of life.

An awkward time comes when life is dominated

by three; it must be reduced to one or increased to four. Three, or that consciousness represented by three, can not long be endured in its intensity and drivenness. If one finds himself in a paralyzing dilemma, he must make the forward thrust to attain an enlightened place of insight, the fourness, or else reduce his consciousness just to survive.

Dr. Jung spent much of his later years working at the symbolism of three and four. He felt that mankind was just evolving from that stage of consciousness represented by three to that represented by four. In 1948 and 1949 he was jubilant at the new dogma of the Catholic church which placed the Virgin Mary with the Trinity, all masculine figures, in Heaven. He felt that this completed an earlier, incomplete stage of development that had brought so much unrest and conflict to the western world. The symbol precedes the fact by many years, which indicates that the possibility is now open to us; but the work is not yet done. Dr. Jung felt that the work of a truly modern person was to make the expansion of consciousness represented by the evolution from three to four—from the consciousness devoted to doing, working, accomplishing, progressing to that characterized by peace, tranquility, existential being. The heart of the matter is that four can contain three, but three can not contain four. A person of the high consciousness of four is capable of all the practicalities of life but is not bound by them. A person of the world of three is not capable of appreciating the elements associated with the number four.

We are apparently in an age where the consciousness of man is advancing from a trinitarian to a quaternarian view. This is one possible and profound way of appraising the extreme chaos our world is now in. One hears many dreams of modern people, who know nothing consciously of this number symbolism, dreaming of three turning into four. This suggests we are going through an evolution of consciousness from the nice orderly all-masculine concept of reality, the trinitarian view of God, toward a quaternarian view that includes the feminine as well as other elements that are difficult to include if one insists on the old values.

It seems that it is the purpose of evolution now to replace an image of perfection with the concept of completeness or wholeness. Perfection suggests something all pure, with no blemishes, dark spots or questionable areas. Wholeness includes the darkness but combines it with the light elements into a totality more real and whole than any ideal. This is an awesome task, and the question before us is whether mankind is capable of this effort and growth. Ready or not, we are in that process.

The year of Mary has come and gone and has mostly been forgotten and seems to have had little immediate effect on our lives. But if we can view this extraordinary event in the right way it will have a profound effect on theology and upon our everyday lives.

When the fourth element is given dignity and honor it is no longer the adversary; it is only when we exclude a psychological truth that it becomes negative or destructive. An element showing its evil side needs only consciousness to give it a useful place in our structure.

Man has often seen the dark side of himself as feminine and, pushing it even further away, has turned it into the witch. Much of the darkness of the rejected element during the Middle Ages was feminine—hence the burning of witches at the stake. These were not a few isolated occurrences that gained unwarranted publicity; it has been estimated that more than four million women were burned at the stake during the height of the counterreformation in Europe. Now, it is a formidable task to incorporate into our personality those elements that were seen to be so dark only a short time ago; to retrieve so dark an element is a dangerous operation. If one has antagonized the wolf at the door he does not suddenly open the door and say, "Now come in."

The Hideous Damsel

Parsifal has conquered so many knights and sent them to Arthur's Court that he has grown famous in the Arthurian world. Now Arthur and his court set forth to find this elusive man of power and search the countryside for him. They find Parsifal one day, set him at the head of the court, and declare a three day festival and tournament in his honor. Parsifal certainly has earned this honor but unwittingly blunders into its inevitable consequence. How many times Parsifal blunders! It is extremely reassuring to see that it is often in his blunders that he finds the next stage of his development. If it were not for this benevolent fact all the Parsifals of the world would have fallen off the edge of the flat world and vanished into the oblivion they deserve. Don Quixote, the archfool of all time, makes his sublime journey entirely by way of nonsense.

At the very height of the three-day festivities a

most hideous damsel appears and puts an instant damper on all the celebration. She is on a decrepit old mule that limped on all four feet. The damsel's black hair was tressed in two braids, "iron dark were her hands and nails." Her closed eyes "small like a rat's." Her "nose like an ape and cat." Her "lips like an ass and bull." "Bearded was she, humpedbreast and back, her loins and shoulders twisted like roots of a tree." Never in royal court was such a damsel seen.

Her mission is to present the other side of the coin at the festival, a task she accomplishes with genius. She recites all Parsifal's sins and stupidities, the worst being his failure to ask the healing question in the Grail castle. Parsifal is humbled and left silent before the court that only a moment before had been praising him to the sky.

With the certainty of sunset the Hideous Damsel will walk into a man's life just when he has reached the apex of his accomplishment.

∽

There is some strange correlation between the achievement of a man and the power of the Hideous Damsel in his life. The greater the height, the greater his capacity for suffering and humiliation seems: the amount of fame and adulation one gets in the outer world seems to determine the sense of failure and meaninglessness he will find at the hands of the Hideous Damsel. One would guess that accomplishment would be the surest protection against meaninglessness, but this is not so. It is the accomplished man who is most capable of asking unanswerable questions about his worth and the meaning of his life. This questioning, often called the "dark night of the soul" in medieval theology, has an uncanny way of claiming one at two or three o'clock in the morning. Someone observed darkly that it is always two A.M. when one is in the "dark night of the soul."

The Hideous Damsel is the carrier of doubt and despair, the destroying, spoiling quality that visits any intelligent man at mid-life. The savor of life has gone; unanswerable questions torment him. "What is the use of going to the office? What difference does it make? What good is it? Why?" Woman pleases him no more, his children are either difficult or gone, vacations don't work any more. Just when he begins to have the time and means for the pleasurable things of life they are no longer meaningful. This is the work of the Hideous Damsel.

There is a great urge in a man at this stage of his life to try to find a new Fair Damsel as protection from the Hideous Damsel; but unless he comes to terms with the dark element first, no old or new damsel of any description will save him from this dark time of his life.

It is genius in a woman if she can be quiet in the presence of her man when he is going through this dark time. This protects her from the projection of the Hideous Damsel that the man would be only too happy to put upon her. A quiet kind of "being there" is the greatest gift a woman can give at this time.

In our tranquilizer age it is the general opinion that the Hideous Damsel time should be avoided and treated as an illness to be cured. To banish her darkness is to sterilize one's chance at the evolution she brings.

This harbinger of darkness accomplishes a profoundly important act of individuation in the court. She parcels out tasks to each of the knights present, each task an individual quest for each knight. Before this moment in evolution all tasks were communal tasks, that is, knights went out in groups or at least in pairs to fight a dragon or lift a siege from a castle. After the visit of the Hideous Damsel all tasks are individual and unique. Each knight has to go alone, find his own path, make a solitary battle in his quest. Collective or group solutions to problems cease here. This change in basic attitude is the only workable answer to the despair brought by the Hideous Damsel. When a man knows that he is alone, unique and on a solitary quest he will be out of that dark time of the Hideous Damsel. All psychological suffering (or happiness, taken in its usual sense) is a matter of comparison. When one accepts the solitariness of his journey there is no comparison possible and he is in that existential world where things simply "are." In this realm there is no happiness or unhappiness in the usual sense but only that state of being that is correctly called Ecstasy. It is bitter on the tongue to admit that this is the gift of the Hideous Damsel but there is no other carrier of so sublime a gift. Perhaps this was known to the author of the medieval statement that "Suffering is the swiftest steed to redemption."

To honor the Hideous Damsel and accept her new view of the nature of the quest is to embark on the second half of one's life.

From the Hideous Damsel Parsifal learns that his task in this new dispensation is to find the Grail castle a second time. He vows he will not sleep twice in the same bed until he finds the visionary world again.

The Hideous Damsel reminds the court that the search for the Grail requires chastity of the knights, and then she limps off, her task accomplished.

For the hundredth time I remind you that the chastity required for this journey has nothing to do with one's conduct with flesh-and-blood women— which has its own laws and requires its own intelligence. The chastity required of a man in this quest is that he neither seduce nor be seduced by the inner woman in terms of mood or anima. All the knights except Parsifal (and Galahad in the English version of the grail Legend) fail in their quest. This is to say that there will be many failures in one's life quest but it is absolutely necessary that consciousness (Parsifal) stay true to the quest. Perfection or a good score is not required; but consciousness is.

The Long Quest

Parsifal spends many years, most of the legends say twenty, on his knightly adventures. He grows more bitter, more disillusioned; he grows farther away from his beloved Blanche Fleur; he forgets why he wields his sword in his knight's journey. He functions with less and less understanding and joy.

These are the dry years of a man's middle age. He knows less and less why he is functioning and is apt to give an evasive answer when asked about the meaning of his life.

Parsifal comes upon a band of ragged pilgrims who are wandering on the road. They say to him, "What are you doing riding in full armor on this, the day of the death of our Lord? Don't you know it is Good Friday? Come with us to the forest hermit, say your confession, and be shriven in preparation for Easter Sunday." Parsifal is suddenly wakened from his dark reverie, and, more from inertia than inspiration, goes with the pilgrims to the old hermit.

THE HERMIT WITHIN

The hermit is the highly introverted part of one's nature that has been waiting and storing energy in a far off corner waiting for this very moment. Extroversion is the usual dominant of the first half of one's life and that is correct. But when one's extroversion has run its race and taken one on that very valuable part of life journey—then one must consult the hermit deep inside for the next step. We do this very badly in our culture and few people know how to draw upon the genius of their introvert nature for the next step. It frequently happens to a modern person that he is forced into his introversion by an illness or accident or paralyzing symptom of some other kind. The hermit is a noble figure and will serve you well if you can go to him in honor and dignity. There is little dignity left if one is dragged into his realm by accident or illness; but one way or another he will have you sometime about the middle of your journey—dignity or no dignity.

To do justice to the hermit, we must speak at least briefly about those whose hermit nature has been so strong that it is the dominant feature of their personality. These few people, born hermits (highly intro-

verted souls), must remain in the forest (sym-
bolically speaking) in solitude, storing up energy so
that they may serve mankind when their quality is
crucial and of the highest value. There are few Red
Knight victories for these persons and they know
little of the laurel leaves of victory. Such people re-
ceive very little encouragement or reinforcement
these days and they often have a lonely and solitary
life to lead. But a day comes when their genius is
absolutely necessary to make a transition to another
stage of life—for themselves or for someone in their
environment. Just to know of this validity is a safeguard for such a person. Please be good to your own
hermit quality or the born hermit in your circle of
friends. If you have a born hermit as a son, don't
push him into Red Knight experiences but let him
find his own forest way.

When Parsifal is with the hermit he finds another
experience much like his exchange with the Hideous
Damsel. Before Parsifal speaks a word, the old hermit, with his clairvoyant quality, berates him with
the long list of his faults and failures. Again, the
worst was his failure to ask the healing question
when he was in the Grail castle.

The hermit quickly grows gentle with Parsifal and
takes him to the road with the instruction to go a
short way, turn left, and cross the drawbridge. The
Grail castle is always that close, but it is generally at

mid-adolescence or middle age that it easily opens to one.

Here the great French poem by Crétien stops! Some guess that he died at this point or that some of the manuscript was lost. I think it is more likely that the author stopped at this point because he had no more to say. That great story from the collective unconscious had gone thus far in its evolution and the author had the humility to stop when he had no more to say. I think the myth has proceeded little further, collectively speaking, to this very day. It is an unfinished story within us, full of power, and begs for further work. If you wish for a true knight's task, take up the story inside yourself where it now lies unfinished and proceed with it. Truly, everyone is Parsifal and his journey is one's own journey.

Other authors have tried to finish the story with indifferent success. We can take up one such continuation and carry Parsifal to his second visit to the Grail castle.

The Grail castle is always just down the road and a turn to the left. If anyone is humble enough and of good heart, he can find that interior castle. Parsifal has had the arrogance beaten out of him by twenty years of fruitless searching, and he is now ready for his castle.

THE SECOND GRAIL CASTLE

Just down the road, turn left, and cross the draw-bridge, which snaps closed ticking the back hooves of your horse. It is always dangerous to make the transition of levels that entry to the Grail castle involves.

Parsifal finds the same ceremonial procession going on; a fair damsel carries the sword that pierced the side of Christ, another damsel carries the paten from which the last supper was served, yet another maiden bears the Grail itself. The wounded Fisher King lies groaning on his litter, poised between life and death in his suffering.

Now, wonder of wonders, with twenty years of maturity and experience behind him, Parsifal asks the question which is his greatest contribution to mankind: Whom does the Grail serve?

What a strange question! Hardly comprehensible to modern ears! In essence the question is the most profound question one can ask: where is the center of gravity of a human personality; or where is the center of meaning in a human life? Most modern people, asked this question in understandable terms for our time, would reply that *I* am the center of gravity; *I* work to improve my life; *I* am working toward my goals; *I* am increasing my equity; *I* am making something of myself—or most common of

77

all—*I* am searching for happiness, which is to say that I want the Grail to serve me. We ask this great cornucopia of nature, this great feminine outpouring of all the material of the world—the air, the sea, the animals, the oil, the forests, and all the productivity of the world—we ask that it should serve us. But no sooner is the question asked than the answer comes reverberating through the Grail castle halls—the Grail serves the Grail King. Again, a puzzling answer. Translated, this means that life serves what a Christian would call God, Jung calls the Self, or and we call by the many terms we have devised to indicate that which is greater than ourselves.

Another language, less poetic but perhaps easier, is available. Dr. Jung speaks of the life process as being the relocation of the center of gravity of the personality from the ego to the Self. He sees this as the life work of a man and the center of meaning for all human endeavor. When Parsifal learns that he is no longer the center of the universe—not even his own little kingdom—he is free of his alienation and the Grail is no longer barred from him. Though he may come and go from the Grail castle during the rest of his life, now he will never be alien to it again.

Even more astonishing, the wounded Fisher King rises, healed, in triumph and joy. The miracle has happened, and the legend of his healing has been accomplished. In Wagner's opera, *Parsifal,* the wounded Fisher King rises at this moment and sings a wondrous song of triumph and power and strength. It is the culmination of the whole tale!

Now who is the Grail King whom we have not heard mentioned before? He is the true king of the realm and he lives in the center of the Grail castle. He lives only on the Host and the Wine of the Grail. He is a thinly disguised figure of God, the earthly representation of the Divine, or in Jungian terms, the Self. It is humbling to learn that we hear of this inner center only when we are ready for it and when we have done our duty of formulating a coherent question.

The object of life is not happiness, but to serve God or the Grail. All of the Grail quests are to serve God. If one understands this and drops his idiotic notion that the meaning of life is personal happiness, then one will find that elusive quality immediately at hand.

This same motif appears in a contemporary myth, *The Fellowship of the Ring* by J. R. R. Tolkien; the power must be taken from those who would exploit it. In the Grail myth the source of power is given to the representative of God. In Tolkien's myth the ring of power is taken from evil hands that would use its power to destroy the world and is put back into the ground from which it came. Earlier myths often spoke of the discovery of power and its emergence from the earth into human hands. Recent myths speak of returning the source of power to the earth or into the Hands of God before we destroy ourselves with it.

One detail in the story is worth special observation: Parsifal need only *ask* the question; he does not have to answer it. When one is discouraged and certain he will never have the intelligence to find the answer to insoluble riddles, he can remember that although it is the duty of the ego to ask a well-formulated question, he is not required to answer it. To ask well is virtually to answer.

Rejoicing bursts forth in the Grail castle; the Grail is brought forth, it gives its food to everyone, including the now-healed Fisher King, and there is perfect peace, joy, and well-being.

Such a dilemma! If you ask the Grail to give you happiness, that demand precludes happiness. But if you serve the Grail and the Grail King properly, you will find that what happens and happiness are the same thing. A play on words becomes the definition of enlightenment.

An identical theme is found in very different language in the "Ten Oxherding Pictures" from Zen Buddhism. This is a series of ten pictures prescribed for an artist to portray the steps toward enlightenment. In the first the young hero searches for the ox—his inner nature; in the second he sees the footprints of the ox; in the third he sees the ox. The series proceeds to the ninth picture in which the hero tames the ox, forges a peaceful relationship with it, and sits quietly surveying the scene. The question rises at this point—Behold the streams flowing, whither nobody knows; and the flowers vividly red—for whom are they? Author Mokusen Miyuki reflects that these words could be translated literally into "The stream flows on its own accord, and the flower is red on its own accord." The Chinese term *tsu,* "of its own accord," is used as a compound, *tsu-jan,* in Taoist thought. It can mean "naturalness," an occurring of the creative spontaneity of nature, within and without. In other words, *tsu-jan,* can be taken psychologically as the living reality of self-realization or the creative urge of the Self manifesting itself in nature.

The series of pictures culminates in the tenth when the hero, now perfectly at peace, walks unnoticed through the village streets. There is nothing extraordinary about him now except that all the trees burst into blossom as he passes by.

This questioning of the meaning of the stream or the redness of the rose from such a different source as Zen Buddhism enhances our understanding of this quest.

A Frenchman, Alexis de Tocqueville, came to America more than a century ago and made some astute observations about the American way. He said that we have a misleading idea at the very head of our Constitution: the pursuit of happiness. One can not pursue happiness; if he does he obscures it. If he will proceed with the human task of life, the relocation of the center of gravity of the personality to something greater outside itself, happiness will be the outcome.

In this year of our Lord we are just beginning to ask the Grail question: do we have the right to cut down the trees, impoverish the soil, and kill all the pelicans? The answer is beginning to come clear; the first lisping syllables of the question are audible. If we can hear this old tale of an innocent fool blundering into the Grail castle for the first time and earning his way there a second time, we can find some sage advice for our own modern way.

SUGGESTIONS FOR FURTHER READING

Bolen, Jean Shinoda. *Gods in Everyman.* San Francisco: Harper & Row, 1989.

Campbell, Joseph. *The Hero with a Thousand Faces.* Princeton: Princeton University Press, 1968.

Jung, Carl G. *Man and His Symbols.* Garden City, N.Y.: Doubleday, 1969.

————. *Memories, Dreams, Reflections.* New York: Random House, Inc., 1961.

Jung, Emma, and Von Franz, Marie-Louise. *The Grail Legend.* A C. G. Jung Foundation Book. New York: G.P. Putnam's Sons, 1970.

Kelsey, Morton T. *Encounter with God.* Minneapolis, Minn.: Bethany Fellowship, Inc., 1972.

Sanford, John A. *The Man Who Wrestled with God.* Ramsey, N.J.: Paulist Press, 1981.

Sanford, John A., and Lough, George. *What Men Are Like.* Ramsey, N.J.: Paulist Press, 1981.

Whitmont, Edward, C. *The Symbolic Quest.* Princeton: Princeton University Press, 1978.